You Love Dogs
We love Dogs

DAVID BOBKER

ISBN: 9798613342136

CONTENTS

FOREWORD

The evidence that people form strong attachments with their pets, especially dogs, is briefly reviewed before identifying the characteristics of such relationships, which include pets being a source of security as well as the objects of caregiving.

In evolutionary terms, dogs' ownership poses a problem, since attachment and devoting resources to another species are, in theory, fitness-reducing.

Dogs keeping is placed into the context of other forms of interspecific associations. Dogs are viewed as manipulating human responses that had evolved to facilitate human relationships, primarily (but not exclusively) those between parent and child.

The precise mechanisms that enable dogs to elicit caregiving from humans are elaborated. They involve features that provide the initial attraction, such as mental characteristics, and those that enable the human owner to derive continuing satisfaction from interacting with the dog, such as the attribution of mental processes to human-like organisms.

These mechanisms can, in some circumstances, cause dog owners to derive more satisfaction from their dog relationship than those with humans, because they supply a type of unconditional relationship that is usually absent from those with other human beings.

From vital role and close relationship between dogs and human as above, this book was born for the goal of expressing reasons and ways you and your dog loves each other in your special and adorable life.

Believe this book's ways, you get the most optimal sentiment from your dog!

UNCONDITIONAL LOVE

We all know our pets love us, but what is behind their unconditional love.

Anyone who has ever owned a pet knows they have the capacity for the kind of unconditional love that is seen otherwise only between a human and its offspring.

The gentle nudge of a wet nose or a lick on the hand comes unbidden when we're upset or feeling down. The bounding dash to the door to greet us is also a demonstrable sign of the strength of the human–canine bond, in particular.

A subtle change in our demeanor can be picked up and registered by our dogs or cats. Cats, although fiercely independent by nature, do possess a similar capacity for love and nurture, as my cat-owning friends can testify.

Studies have also shown that looking a dog in the eyes can boost levels of oxytocin (a hormone involved in social bonding), in both the person and the dog. It's not just "cupboard love" triggered by a hungry belly. There is in fact nothing artificial that could ever replace that sheer authenticity of feeling. Dogs are the only species that, like a human child, runs to its human when it is frightened, anxious or just pleased to see us.

It is also the only animal, aside from other humans, that actively seeks out eye contact with people, and truly wants to be with us. Cats too come to us when we are down and will show they are pleased to see us with a lick on the hand or a gentle purr to express their own feelings of contentment.

Pets give people so much in terms of love and emotional support. Simply stroking a dog, cat, rabbit or even horse can lead to lower blood pressure and can combat stress. The feelings are reciprocated, as our touch can have therapeutic effects for our pets, particularly if they are feeling out of sorts.

Companion animals can provide support and friendship to society's lonely, sick or elderly. They can be friends to those who do not easily understand the world around them. Autistic children for instance can be guided gently from their closed, confusing and isolated worlds by a patient and loving dog or cat. Anxiety disorders and depression also can be eased by the loving presence of a pet.

Sophie and Nell, my Cavalier King Charles Spaniels, instinctively know when I am under pressure or upset about something. They know what a "hug" and a "stroke" mean, and offer both eagerly.

The wider bond between people and dogs has strengthened over time, around 30,000 years to be precise. Canines have the unique ability to pick up on how we are feeling according to various studies, and similar research is being carried out with cats. For example, animal cognition scientists at Emory University in the US trained dogs to lie still in an MRI machine and used fMRI (functional magnetic resonance imaging) to track their neural responses to the smell of people and dogs, both familiar and unknown. Because dogs navigate the world through their noses, the way they process smell offers a lot of potential insight into how they interact with the world around them.

The scientists found that dog owners' aroma actually sparked activation in the "reward center" of their brains, called the caudate nucleus. This effectively found that canines have the ability to distinguish between us and the huge amount of other olfactory stimuli around them.

In Budapest, researchers at Eotvos Lorand University studied canine brain activity in response to different human and dog sounds, including voices, barks and the meaningful grunts and sighs both species emit. Researchers discovered that happy sounds in particular light up the auditory cortex in both people and dogs. This strengthens the argument that humans and canines have a uniquely strong and resilient bond.

Many people rail against the increasing "humanization" of our pets, but I think that's wrong. People aren't generally trying to turn their pets into little humans. They are instead seeing companion animals increasingly as loving, sentient creatures that, as even science has proven, truly love us. Our pets deserve human-grade food, a warm and safe place to rest, plenty of exercise and our unconditional love and attention.

Perhaps it is a sign of the good side of our human natures that we are increasingly willing to provide these things?

That, by itself, says something about the bond that humans and dogs share. We live with cats, we work with horses, we hire cows for their milk and chickens for their eggs and pay them with food—unless we kill them and eat them instead. Our lives are entangled with those of other species, but we could disentangle if we wanted.

With dogs, things are different. Our world and their world swirled together long ago like two different shades of paint. Once you've achieved a commingled orange, you are never going back to red and yellow.

But why is that? It is not enough to say that the relationship is symbiotic— that dogs hunt for us and herd for us and we keep them warm and fed in return. Sharks and remora fish struck a similarly symbiotic deal, with the remora cleaning parasites from the shark's skin and getting to help itself to scraps from the shark's kills as its pay. That underwater deal is entirely transactional; love plays no part. Humans and dogs, by contrast, adore each other.

The relationship began—well, nobody knows exactly when it began. The earliest remains of humans and dogs interred together date to 14,000 years ago, but there are some unconfirmed finds that are said to be more than twice as old. The larger point is the meaning of the discoveries: we lived with dogs and then chose to be buried with them. Imagine that.

It was only by the tiniest bit of genetic chance that our cross-species union was forged at all. Dogs and wolves share 99.9% of their mitochondrial DNA—the DNA that's passed down by the mother alone—which makes the two species nearly indistinguishable. But elsewhere in the genome, there are a few genetic scraps that make a powerful difference. On chromosome six in particular, investigators have found three genes that code for hyper-sociability—and they are in the same spot as similar genes linked to similar sweetness in humans.

Our ancestors didn't know what genes were many millennia ago, but they did know that every now and then, one or two of the midsize scavengers with the long muzzles that came nosing around their campfires would gaze at them with a certain attentiveness, a certain loving neediness, and that it was awfully hard to resist them. So they welcomed those few in from the cold and eventually came to call them dogs, while the animals' close kin that did not pull the good genes—the ones we would come to call wolves or jackals or coyotes or dingoes—would be left to make their way in the state of nature in which they were born.

When humans ourselves left the state of nature, our alliance with dogs might well have been dissolved. If you didn't need a working dog—and fewer and fewer people did—the ledger went out of balance. We kept paying dogs their food-and-¬shelter salary, but we got little that was tangible in return. Never mind, though; by then we were smitten.

Our language reflected how love-drunk we'd gotten: the word "puppy" is thought to have been adapted from the French poupée, or doll—an object on which we lavish irrational affection. Our folk stories were populated by dogs: The Africans spoke of Rukuba, the dog who brought us fire; the Welsh told the tale of the faithful hound Gelert, who saved a prince's baby from a wolf. Aristocrats took to including the family dog in family portraits. Wealthy eccentrics took to including dogs in their wills.

Today, at least in areas populated by humans, dogs are the planet's most abundant terrestrial carnivore. There are about 900 million of them worldwide, just shy of 80 million of whom live in the U.S. alone. The single species that is the domestic dog—*Canis lupus familiaris*—has been subdivided into hundreds of breeds, selected for size or temperament or color or cuteness.

The average American dog owner spends more than $2,000 a year on food, toys, medical care and more, and some people would be prepared to pay a much higher, much dearer price. When Hurricane Katrina struck New Orleans in 2005, so many people refused to evacuate without their dogs that Congress passed a law requiring disaster preparedness plans to make accommodations for pets.

What began as a mutual-services contract between two very different species became something much more like the love, none of that makes a lick of sense, but it doesn't have to. Love rarely touches the reasoning parts of the brain. It touches the dreamy parts, the devoted parts—it touches the parts we sometimes call the heart. For many thousands of years, it is there that our dogs have lived.

WHY DO WE LOVE PETS?

Ours is a pet-loving culture. What has become known as "human-animal interactions?

Researchers spend a lot of time exploring what has become known as "human-animal interactions," and the pet industry spends a lot of money promoting what it prefers to call the "human-animal bond." But that concept might have been laughable a century ago, when animals served a more utilitarian role in our lives. And it was "deeply unfashionable" among scholars as recently as the 1980s, as John Bradshaw writes in his new book, "The Animals Among Us: How Pets Make Us Human."

Bradshaw, an honorary research fellow at the University of Bristol in England, would know. He was trained as a biologist — one who began by studying animals, not people, and not their relationship. But he says his work on dog and cat behavior led him to conclude that he would never fully understand those topics without also considering how humans think about their animals. In 1990, he and a small group of other researchers who studied pet ownership coined a term for their field. Today, university students at a few dozen U.S. universities study the topic he helped pioneer.

Bradshaw argues that our fascination with pets is not because they are useful, nor even because they are cute, and certainly not because they will make us live longer. Instead, he writes, pet-keeping is an intrinsic part of human nature, one rooted deeply in our own species' evolution.

There are loads of press releases and read lots of headlines about how pets make us healthy, but the science is quite a bit fuzzier.

There is evidence that interacting with pets does reduce people's stress, provided the pet is behaving properly. Good interactions do have quite a profound effect, causing changes in oxytocin and in beta endorphins. Those are actual changes going on in the body of somebody who is stroking a friendly dog. So that is the upside.

The downside is that pets, real pets that actually live with people, cause stress and expense and all sorts of other things that can cause arguments within the family. And if you take humanity as a whole, I suspect that those two things kind of balance out. For every paper that says that pets make you live longer or that they make people healthier, many other reports — particularly those that come from medical professionals, who don't really have a stake in the field — that find no effect or actually negative effects. The reporting bias is in favor of the good ones, so the study that showed that cat owners were usually more depressed than people who don't have any pets didn't rate any headlines. So pet-keeping as a habit, averaged out, is probably not having any major effect on health in either direction. If the dog gets people out and about and likes energetic exercise, then there are probably health benefits.

But they are not just going to come as part of the package.

Why is there such a mismatch in public perception about pets as a panacea and the evidence for it?

It is about a puzzling and unusually unique effect pets give to people, which is what I call the trustworthiness effect, which has not received a huge amount of attention in the press, but it has been replicated in studies in several different countries.

People with animals, or as simply described as having a friendly dog with them, instantly become more trustworthy in the eyes of the person who's encountering that person or having that person described to them. I think it actually explains quite a lot — people are believed when they tell nice stories about animals. Whether that applies to news reports as well, I'm just guessing, but I think it's a reasonable explanation. I think it also explains a lot of the effects of animal-assisted therapy. The magic is actually in making the person with the animal much more approachable. In a senior residence, it's not simply the seniors who find the visitor a good person to talk to, but the staff finds the visits beneficial as well. It makes the whole place seem a bit homelier.

The dog, or whatever animal, is changing people's perception of the person doing the therapy. This is the trustworthiness factor, and it explains quite a lot of our biases.

What is the harm if people have mistaken beliefs about pets? Lots of animals need homes.

There are some potential risks. The one that we are seeing most is people bypassing the idea that you have to know about these animals.

50 or 100 years ago, the knowledge of how to look after animals was passed from person to person. Now we are much more insular. And the idea that simply getting a pet is going to make you happy and sorrowful does not work if you don't do the homework about what the animal needs. One trend which I have particular concern about is for flat-faced dogs. People don't really understand that having a dog that looks very cute is also likely to have breathing difficulties, eye problems and other health issues. I find that quite distressing. We have a lot of knowledge now about how dogs think and how they feel, and yet that knowledge is still not getting through to a particular kind of owner who is just obeying the fashion and their gut instincts. They are told that this is going to be a really good experience for them, and maybe

it is, but it probably will not be that great an experience for the dog.

Flat-faced dogs like this bulldog puppy, posing at an American Kennel Club event in 2013, are among the most popular breeds in the United States.

Why do we keep getting pets?

One answer is that there is this satisfaction — stroking a dog or a cat causes hormones to be released and makes the person doing it feel good. You can trace that back to our very ancient history as hairy primates. Grooming one another is the main glue that holds most primate societies together. Now we have got other ways of socializing, but somewhere deep in our brains is a need to do this grooming of something that's hairy, and we can satisfy that by stroking a dog or combing the cat.

We also have to explain why it's persisted when we'd have more money if we didn't have pets. I think it used to be adaptive — people who were seen to be good with animals were more accepted by other people in their tribe, and there may have even been some selection for brides and grooms based on affinity with animals. Second, domestication of animals has been a very important aspect of the emergence of what we call civilization. But it's actually intrinsically improbable, because to domesticate an animal you have to change its genetics. Even nowadays that takes many generations.

The only way you can account for the separation of domestic animals from their wild ancestors, and the only way they stopped interbreeding, is because the domestic animals, the ones that were slightly tamer, were people's pets and so were physically and emotionally and culturally separated. So we had the emergence of a domestic dog, which is useful, a domestic cat, which can be useful because it hunts around houses, and goats and sheep that you can herd and milk. Pet-keeping became an advantage, because the societies that were good at it and wanted to do it domesticated animals before other neighboring societies and groups of people.

These days, we spend lots of money to keep pets alive, we send them to spas and we buy them furniture. How did things go from pet-keeping to pet indulgence?

If you look at accounts of the pets owned by royalty and nobility back in the Middle Ages, you'll find dogs and cats and monkeys and birds that were treated very, very well and fed very choice food. They weren't dressed up for Halloween, because Halloween hadn't been invented, but I think the habit of doing this is actually quite ancient. It's much more widespread now just because people have the resources. But there are other trends going on as well. In the U.K., we are seeing that people are delaying having families. If it's not possible for somebody to have a child, or they feel that they're not ready because they haven't achieved what they wanted in their career, or they can only afford a small apartment and feel that a child should have a house with a yard, then I think that gap can be filled by an animal for a few years. It's a lot cheaper to buy your dog a Halloween costume than to get an apartment with one more room in it.

What Is the future of pet-keeping look like?

If we assume that affluence continues to spread, which is debatable, I would see many other cultures becoming more keen to have pets. I did some studies 15 or 20 years ago looking at the emergence of the Americanization of pet-keeping in Japan, where increasingly younger people are bringing dogs into the house and treating them more like members of the family. I think that will spread to other cultures. Longer term, there will need to be a rethink because of world resources. Both dogs and cats are carnivores — the cat is a very strict carnivore. The idea that we can continue to essentially farm the world in a way that provides enough meat for dogs and cats to eat, let alone humans, is probably not sustainable. Whether it will be possible for people to continue to keep these animals, or what kinds of substitutes they find if it does become impossible, I think is going to be fascinating, if somewhat painful for the people involved.

What "anthrozoology" topics need more exploration?

A lot of research in "anthrozoology" is narrowed down to making it a kind of branch of alternative medicine. There is a lot of people looking for health benefits, a lot of people thinking of animals as therapeutic agents. I think the more interesting questions are about how people perceive animals, what kind of emotions do animals cause in people, and why do they do that? Pet-keeping is pretty irrational, at least in one way of looking at it. So let's look at that rather than looking at the therapeutic benefits, which the evidence suggests are far less powerful than the most enthusiastic proponents would have us believe.

Also, how does our relationship with animals living in our houses affect the way we perceive the natural environment? The arguments about the planet and what we should do with it tend to focus on logic. Not enough is made of people's day-to-day contact with animals. You can educate children a lot more about biology — rather than the stuff they get on a screen — by just pointing out to them, 'This is a dog. This is how it lives and breathes, how it digests its food.' There is evidence that if you do that, you not only teach kids to be better pet owners, but you teach them to be more empathetic toward animals in general. We need to have a new generation of people who care very passionately about animals, and I believe that pets are a good way to do that, rather than being second-class animals or even, as in the controversy over cats killing wildlife, perceived as the opposite. That is very unhelpful, because people who actually understand cats are probably the same people who are supporting the conservation of wildlife.

DO OUR PETS REALLY LOVE US?

We dote on our cats and dogs, but is it a one-way relationship?

Here is what science tells us about how to decode their emotions, whether they are avoiding us or getting a little too amorous with our legs.

It is almost a year to the day since Dustin, our milky-eyed nerve-bag of a cat, died and we still miss him a great deal, although he was not a great giver of emotion. We miss his refusing to look our way immensely. And his not wanting to be stroked there, there or there. But it wasn't Dustin's fault he was like this. Unknown trauma in kitten-hood (he was left in a shoebox at the front door of a vet's surgery) meant that he lived his entire 11 years in terror of being mauled to death by some unseen enemy. Understandably, this constant fear made Dustin very, very nervous.

Through many years of care and affection, we almost managed to rescue him from this anxiety until – almost as if to prove a point – Dustin was mauled to death by two pet dogs off the lead. When we pulled his frozen body out of the freezer before his funeral, Dustin had a withering expression – "I told you so" it seemed to say. This was the only time we really got to stroke him properly. Frozen solid.

I often find myself wondering whether Dustin loved us. The shamefully needy part of me wants reassurance that we made his 11 years as pleasurable as possible. But can we ever really understand what pets feel for us? After a year of this topic swirling around in my head, I thought I would share where I have got to.

First, some definitions. There is something very British about the fact we have many, many words to describe types of falling moisture (mist, drizzle, hail, sleet, etc.) and yet the most dramatic and powerful of emotions – motivating billions of humans to do extraordinary things for one another each day – is chucked into a single bucket labelled, rather blandly, "love". One can't help but feel that the ancient Greeks had it right, by pulling love apart into various strands. *Storge* ("store-gae") is the love between family members, for instance; *eros* is erotic love; *philia* is something like the loyalty that friendship brings; *philautia* is love for the self. And so, in this piece, I would like to break the concept of pet love into these neat and easily digestible Greek chunks.

To storge, familial love. It won't surprise you to learn that dogs, more than any other pet, exhibit oodles of this form of love for us. And, unlike most other pets, these attachments have been the subject of many scientific studies. The science confirms what we knew all along, that most dogs actively choose proximity to humans and, within a few months of being born, a puppy's attraction is clearly toward people rather than other dogs. Dogs exhibit varying degrees of separation anxiety when their humans temporarily leave them. Blood pressure rates in dogs lower when they are being stroked by us. It is a form of storge that we share with one another. No question.

Studies of brain chemicals add further weight to this relationship. In dogs and humans (in fact all mammals) the behaviors that bond individuals are maintained through a cocktail of molecules that are absorbed in different ways by the brain. Many of these are regulated by brain hormones that include vasopressin and oxytocin, the (dramatically over-hyped) "love" molecule. In all mammals (including humans) production of this hormone spikes when individuals are sexually aroused, while giving birth and while nursing offspring. It also rises when we see those that we love, particularly close family members. Interestingly, dogs respond with an oxytocin surge not only when interacting with one another, but also (unlike nearly all other mammals) when interacting with humans.

A similar phenomenon occurs with cats. <u>One small-scale study</u> suggests that cats do receive an oxytocin boost upon being petted by their owners, so there may be love there, but it reflects one-fifth of the amount seen in dogs. If anything sums up cats, it is this.

But what of eros? Thankfully, most dogs or cats don't view us in an erotic light. Even leg-humping isn't likely to be a sex thing. The intentions of a horny dog may not necessarily be to inseminate their owner's leg, but instead to manage unresolved tensions within the human-canine household. Some argue it could be about dominance; others that it could be to let off steam. There is also a chance that, well, a bit of friendly leg-humping just feels really nice to a dog, but not necessarily in a knowing, sexual way. The behavior is seen in male and female dogs, and, occasionally, in cats.

Birds, however, are another story. Birds are far more likely to feel a warmth for their owners that you could term eros. A parrot that is tenderly stroked in the wrong places by its minder, for instance, will often misread friendship signals as foreplay and begin producing sex hormones. Should you wish not to sexually excite a parrot, try not to stroke down its back or on, or under, its wings. These are the areas that males and females preen in the early stages of their courtship in the wild. A stroke like this is like the kiss and a cuddle that readies them for sex. Upon discovering this fact, I realized I had more than once inadvertently sexed up a parrot.

Ancient Greeks had no word for cupboard love, but, undoubtedly, this is a love the vast majority of animal pets may feel for us. The pet frog or snake that readies itself from its slumber when the humans appear with food. The fish that swarm to the top of a tank at feeding time. Even invertebrates such as stick insects and hissing cockroaches might approach something like this form of love. And you really could argue that it's a kind of love – something close to philia, a loyalty or a dependable friendship, with the emphasis on food dependability. Sure, it's not a love that inspires sonnets, but it's something.

A desperately depressed part of me wonders if Dustin loved only himself – that he exhibited philautia. That his each and every day was consumed with where best to hide, how best to be fed and how best to maintain the status quo of survival. This is the ultimate slap in the face for self-obsessed human caregiver like me, and so considering Dustin in this way naturally saddens me. But then I remember something wonderful. Rare moments of … something else.

Every few months, when he thought we were fast asleep, a very different Dustin would show himself to us – but he would only emerge in the darkest of night. Dustin would sit on the end of the bed and he would watch me sleep. As I lay on my front, he would wait a few minutes before making a stealthy approach and he would begin to pummel his paws against my ribs. A deep purr would emanate from his broad body. This choking purr moved my bones as I held my eyes closed. Minute after minute, he would go on like this, purring and pummeling, and then he would change position. He would lie down and rest his chin in the cleft between my shoulder blades and stretch his paws over my shoulders as if cuddling me.

I would lie there motionless, eager not to ruin these rare and magical moments, breathing in the rhythmic vibrations of his deep purrs. Sometimes, a long, sinuous blob of gelatinous pleasure-drool would roll down my neck. I didn't care. I wore it as a badge of honor. But then it would end. After about 20 minutes, the spell would lift. Dustin would run out of the door, apparently disgusted with himself for exposing his emotion so wantonly. I don't think the ancient Greeks had a word for a love like that. A love like that is hard to pin down, hard to put into words. You know it when it happens, that is as close as I can get to putting it into a sentence.

And so, you loved like you lived, dearest Dustin. Cautiously. Yours was a careful love, but a real and vivid love, nonetheless – a love on a spectrum of incredible ways in which humans engage with other animals on planet Earth and, in fleeting moments or in lifelong infatuation, they engage back.

ADORABLE WAYS
YOUR DOG EXPRESSES LOVE

Your dog becomes a boisterous new member of your family.

When you get a dog, your life changes. Your dog becomes a boisterous new member of your family. He probably eats in your kitchen, and maybe he sleeps on your couch. He might take over your yard and, if he's not too loud, charm your neighbors. He wins you over with his adorable dog behavior and pure happiness when you walk in the door.

Another thing that happens the day you get a dog? You become a dog owner. Sure, that means you're responsible for all the messes he makes. But it also means you become obsessed with figuring out what your dog is feeling. You find yourself constantly guessing at the motivation behind his dog behavior. And at least once in a while, you'll try to figure out whether your dog loves you. Here are the ways his dog behavior might tell you.

1. He uses the right body language

The New York Times reports that your dog's body language is a clear sign he loves you. Most of us know some of the obvious body-language signs. Do your dog's ears perk up when you walk in the room? Does he wriggle around excitedly when you open the front door? Or does his tail wag vigorously? That means he's happy, as does a more recently discovered feature of dog body language. "When dogs feel fundamentally positive about something or someone, their tails wag more to the right side of their rumps," according to the New York Times. "When they have negative feelings, their tail wagging is biased to the left."

2. He stays close to you

Tail-wagging isn't the only clue your dog loves you. Vet-Street reports that many dogs lean against their owners. Some stand on your feet. They might stay close to you during a walk. And when they take a nap, they might want to cuddle as close to you as possible. The reason why? Your dog wants affection from you. "Dogs love to cuddle," according to Vet-Street. "And if the person you want to cuddle with is always sitting and standing, then cuddling takes the form of leaning on her or sitting on her shoes as she taps away at the keyboard."

3. He makes eye contact

Does your dog stare into your eyes? It turns out that's one of the ways that he says, "I love you." According to Science Magazine, researchers have determined "mutual gazing" between dogs and their owners causes significant increases in oxytocin. Oxytocin in both humans and dogs is a powerful hormone that plays a significant role in bonding. Science Magazine reports, "The results suggest that human-dog interactions elicit the same type of oxytocin positive feedback loop as seen between mothers and their infants."

4. He responds to your voice

Sure, your dog runs over when you tell him that dinner is served or it's time for a walk. But according to NPR, researchers have determined the reward pathways in a dog's brain light up when they hear praising words and approving intonations. Your dog is listening to what you're saying and how you're saying it. Dogs process speech by separating the meaning of the words from the intonation. And they analyze each aspect of speech independently. If your dog runs over to you when you call him or responds positively to the sound of your voice, that's a pretty good sign that he loves you.

5. He raises his left eyebrow when you walk into the room

You've probably realized if your dog wags his tail or turns his head when you walk into the room he's happy to see you. But researchers have discovered another interesting behavior. They recorded dogs' facial expressions with high-speed cameras and found dogs raise their left eyebrows when they see their owners. The dogs didn't raise their eyebrows to just any positive stimuli. For instance, they didn't raise their eyebrows when they saw an attractive toy. So the researchers concluded the eyebrow lift likely reflects "the dog's attachment to the owner."

6. He yawns after you do

Another surprising sign your dog loves you? He yawns after you do. Researchers found dogs catch human yawns. They explained that so-called continuous (or contagious) yawning relates to the capacity for empathy. And they demonstrated that dogs yawn in response to human yawns. So if your dog seems to yawn in response to yours, he's likely demonstrating that he can read your emotional signals and empathize with you.

7. He prefers a belly rub to a treat

Whether you're training a young dog or just expressing your love to an adult canine, you might wonder how to best reward your dog. According to Science Magazine, a study found dogs respond more positively to praise than to food. Many dogs even prefer a belly rub from their owners than a treat. Sure, some dogs react more strongly to food. But if your dog wants attention more than he wants a treat, that's a pretty good sign he values your attention. Science Magazine explains, "The study supports how important social interaction is to dogs — and provides a healthier alternative to treats, too."

8. He shows positive emotions toward you

Neuro-economics professor Gregory Berns wrote in The New York Times that after using an MRI to map dogs' brain activity, he came to a fascinating conclusion: "Dogs, and probably many other animals (especially our closest primate relatives), seem to have emotions just like us." Most of us don't have access to an MRI to check out our dog's brain activity. But if your dog seems happy to spend time with you or seems to grow attached to your kids, that might be a pretty good sign your dog loves you and your family.

9. He tries to engage with you

Not sure whether your dog is actually happy to see you or just wants the food and attention you provide? Modern Dog reports five ways your dog tries to engage with you. Does your dog greet you at the door? Perhaps he makes relaxed eye contact with you? Does he cuddle with you when he doesn't want something? Maybe he chooses to be in the same room as you, even if he's sleeping or playing on his own? Or does he take his toys over to you? All of these are signs your dog is trying to engage with you and thinks of you as far more than the provider of his food.

10. He bonds with you like a baby would

CBS News reports that according to scientists, the bond formed between your dog and you might be quite similar to the bond formed between a baby and parents. The bond comes about thanks to the "secure base effect." The idea is infants use their parents as a safe "home base" when they interact with the world around them. If your dog gets distressed and looks for you in unfamiliar situations, he's relying on you in the same way.

11. He chooses to spend time with you

Jeffrey Masson writes in the book, *Dogs Never Lie About Love*, that "once a dog loves you, he loves you always, no matter what you do, no matter what happens, no matter how much time goes by." Humans and dogs can, on a basic level, understand each other's emotional responses. And dogs like to spend time with humans, in Masson's assessment, "because dogs love us."

12. He tries to follow your rules

Clive L. Wynne, director of the Canine Science Collab-oratory at Arizona
State University, tells The New York Times that dogs "have this kind of open
hyper-sociability. The dog itself wants to give out love." Dogs, like humans,
seem to have multiple types of intelligence. Some show empathy. Others
excel at communication. Yet others have great memory. And some show
exceptional reasoning skills. You might want your dog to be smart. But the
New York Times notes that smart dogs aren't always fun to live with. So if
your dog is eager to please you and tries to obey your rules, you know your
dog loves you — even if he isn't the smartest animal on the block.

13. He thinks of you as family

Mic reports that according to brain scans of dogs, our canine companions
not only love us, but think of us as family. When your dog smells your scent,
the reward center of his brain, called the caudate nucleus, lights up. When
you make happy sounds — whether you're speaking, laughing, or making
other sounds — your dog's auditory cortex lights up. He's wired to pick up
on your subtle mood changes.

14. He bonds with you

Humans' brains release a hormone called oxytocin, frequently referred to as "the love hormone," during agreeable human reactions. Your brain releases oxytocin when you see someone you love, when you interact with a friend, or even when a stranger is kind to you. The hormone helps us bond with and care about others. And, interestingly enough, Claremont Graduate University researcher Paul Zak reports for The Atlantic that dogs' brains release oxytocin, too. "That animals of different species induce oxytocin release in each other suggests that they, like us, may be capable of love," Zak says.

15. He's simply being a dog

According to The New Yorker, dogs "domesticated themselves. They chose us." Dogs diverged from wolves when they chose to get close to humans — likely motivated by the free food and shelter. Humans keep them as pets not because they're useful but because they make good companions. This is because they made an "ancestral bet" thousands of years ago to stop hunting and start befriending people for food. So from an evolutionary perspective, a domesticated dog wants to please you. By simply being a dog, your dog is telling you he loves you.

EFFECTIVE WAYS YOU SHOW LOVE

*You can express your true feelings to your dog
that will leave no doubt in their mind about your love and devotion.*

You are absolutely crazy about your dog, and you are not afraid to show it. But all the treats, toys, fancy collars, and comfy beds cannot let your dog know just how special they are to you.

Sure, they appreciate all that stuff, but in order to convey love for your pup, you have to speak their language. But do not worry. Just because you do not speak dog does not mean you cannot convey your love in a way your pup will understand.

Here are a few ways you can express your true feelings to your dog that will leave no doubt in their mind about your love and devotion.

1. Ear Rubs Make Your Dog High On Love

Have you ever scratched behind your dog's ears only to find that they lean into your hand and slowly drift into a sort of doggy trance? That's because ear rubs literally make your dog high.

A dog's ears are full of nerve endings that send impulses all through the body, triggering the release of endorphins. These hormones act as painkillers and are natural "drugs" that are also released when dogs feel love.

When you show your affection for your pups with ear rubs, you can be sure that they're getting the message.

2. Try Feeding Your Dog by Hand

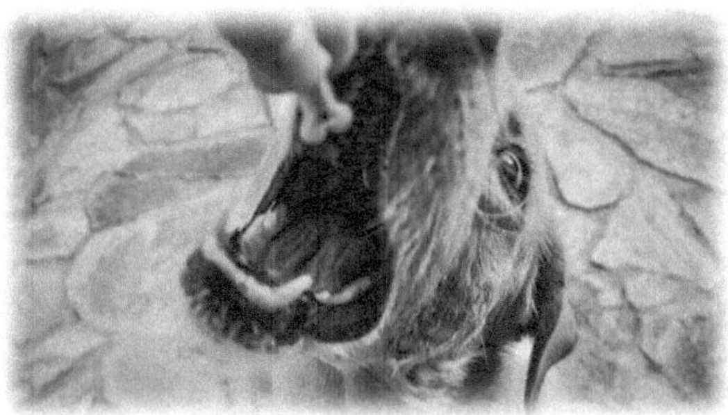

Some experts recommend that, especially with puppies, you try feeding your dog by hand. This not only shows your dog that you are a food provider and reduces food aggression, but it's an intimate experience and creates a strong bond between you and your pup.

As your dog grows older, the need to feed by hand may fade, but offering treats during training is still a great way to show your pup that you care. Just don't overdo it.

3. Just Tell Them You Love Them

A study published in *Science* found that dogs do, in fact, understand some human speech. Dog were studied in an MRI scanner that showed that they experienced the most happiness when they heard not just a praising tone, but words of praise, as well. This suggests that they don't just listen to our tone of voice, but they interpret meaning from words, too. So sometimes just telling your dog how you feel is a great way to express your love.

4. Train Your Dog

Positive reinforcement is an excellent way to communicate your love, and training your dog will give you that opportunity and only make your bond stronger.

It will let you present your dog with their favorite forms of motivation, whether that's food, praise, or play, and your dog will come to see you as a provider of the things they love the most. They'll see that when they work with you, they're making you happy, and your rewards will make them happy in return. When you both work to make each other happy, you're both showing your love for each other.

5. Learn What Your Dog Is Saying

Did you know that many dogs don't like to be hugged? And sometimes they really hate when you approach them directly. And sometimes they're not excited to meet your friends or strangers.

Dogs can express a lot through body language if you know what to look for. By learning how dogs communicate, you can reduce the amount of times they feel stressed and work on making them feel at ease. This will increase their trust for you and build your loving relationship.

When you are their protector, guardian, and friend, you can be sure that your dog will be feeling all the love.

DOG TRAINING

*Training is an excellent way to bond with your dog
and will help you build a good relationship with them.*

A rewarding part of dog ownership is successfully training your dog. Training is an excellent way to bond with your dog and will help you build a good relationship with them.

Whether young or old - all dogs can benefit from learning some basic commands. Our guides can help you with the basics of how to train your dog but we also recommend dog training classes, especially for more advanced methods such as clicker training.

A qualified behaviorist can help with behavioral issues such as excessive barking, aggression, destructiveness and phobias.

But if the basics such as sit, down, stay and leave are what you are looking for - look no further.

What are the benefits of training my dog?

Teaching your dog basic obedience like sit, wait and coming back when called gives them the freedom to do the things they like to do, like running off lead and coming with you to meet friends and family, while being safe and under control.

Dogs are intelligent animals and most love to learn so training can be a great way of stopping them from getting bored.

How do dogs learn?

All training should be reward based. Giving your dog something they really like such as food, toys or praise when they show a particular behavior means that they are more likely to do it again.

It is important to find out what your dog really likes and what their favorite things are. Favorite treats are often small pieces of meat or cheese. The better the reward the more your dog will enjoy training and learning.

Top training tips

- Always start lessons for new tricks in a quiet room in your house away from any distractions

- Break training up into short but regular sessions so your dog is not overwhelmed

- Be patient, just like us, dogs all learn at different rates so do not worry if your dog does not pick things up straight away

- Always end with something your dog knows, so the session finishes positively

- Have fun!

TRICKS TO TEACH YOUR DOG

This chapter show you the ultimate list of dog trick ideas.

Welcome to the Ultimate List of Dog Trick Ideas!

1. Bow

Downward-facing dog is a great stretch and shoulder workout dogs AND people – and it's a super cute trick to teach your dog!

- Start with a treat in your hand and then push it forward between your dog's front legs.

- If he bends his front leg without lowering his rear, he gets the treat. But if he lays down all the way, no treat.

- After 5 repetitions, put start luring your dog with an empty hand instead of a hand with a treat in it. Deliver your treat from a treat pouch instead.

- Start giving the verbal cue ("bow") about 1 second before you do the hand motion. If your dog bows before you lure him, jackpot! Your dog will quickly start realizing that the word "bow" gets him paid really well.

It took a lot of practice to start fading out my hand motion – we got really reliant on it. Whoops! Try to start making your hand motion small ASAP to reduce this problem.

2. Sit Pretty or Beg

This trick is super fun to teach your dog – and it's adorable. This trick isn't a good idea for really big dogs, young dogs, or some dogs with back or hip issues, so keep that in mind.

- Hold a treat or toy above your dog's head so that he lifts his front paws up to look at it or try to reach it.

- Click and give a treat when his paws leave the ground.

- After 5 repetitions, keep your treats in your pouch and just hold out an empty hand – but still reward generously.

- After getting it right 10 times in a row, add a verbal cue. Say the cue right before you give the hand signal.

- Start to shape the behavior by rewarding your dog for "sitting pretty" longer or higher.

- Fade out your hand signal by giving the cue just before the hand signal and rewarding extra-well if your dog gets it without the hand signal.

3. High 5

This adorable trick is one of my favorite tricks to teach a dog! I teach this by teaching shake first, then putting our hands up high for a "high 5."

- Put a tasty treat in your hand and hold it out.

- If your dog paws at your hand, click (or say "good boy") and feed a treat from your OTHER hand.

- Repeat 5 times.

- Remove the treat from your hand and repeat step 2 without treats.

- Repeat 10 times.

- Put your hand higher and higher, until your dog is "high 5-ing" you the way you like.

- Repeat 10 times at the proper height.

- Add a cue by saying "High 5" right before presenting your hand for the high 5.

4. Back Up

This is a useful trick to teach your dog. You can use this trick as part of competitive obedience, as a way to get your dog out of the kitchen, as a way to build your dog's body awareness and agility, and more.

- Sit down in a comfy chair with your knees apart.

- Feed your dog a treat right between your legs.

- When your dog takes a small step backwards (most will right away so they can see you better), click and feed a treat.

- Repeat 5 times, feeding right between your legs and clicking when your dog steps back.

- Now wait for your dog to take 2 steps back before clicking. Repeat 5 times.

- Gradually add more and more steps to your dog's "back up."

- When your dog is readily backing up 4 or 5 paces, add a cue by saying "Back up" right after you feed the treat.

5. Spin

This trick is a great introductory trick to teach your dog. It's far easier than "roll over" and is just as cute!

- Take a treat in your hand and lure the dog in a circle. Feed the dog when he's facing you again.

- Repeat 5 times.

- Repeat the luring motion WITHOUT a treat in your hand. Do this 10 times.
- Feed from your other hand for each successful turn.

- Start to make your luring motion smaller and smaller.

- Add a cue (I use "spin" for a clockwise turn and "whirl" for a counterclockwise one) by saying the cue just before giving the hand signal.

6. Leg Weave

This flashy trick is surprisingly easy to teach. It also helps keep your dog's back limber and is a great side-stretch. Barley and I actually start out most runs with a few leg weaves for his warm up!

- Start to teach by luring your dog through your legs with a cookie.

- Give him the treat after each leg wrap – feed him right in front of your knee.

- After five correct repetitions, leave the treat in your treat pouch and then lead your dog through your legs with an empty hand. Feed after each repetition. This step ensures your dog will listen without the cookie!

- Now start to make your hand movements smaller and add a verbal cue. You'll get there in no time!

7. Car Wash

This dog trick is cute and useful. I've taught this trick for clients whose dogs are nervous around other dogs – some dogs like to get between their owner's legs for comfort. I've also taught this trick to a female jogger who wanted her dog to know how to get between her and strangers.

In this trick, your dog stands between your legs and will move with you when you move. Here's how to teach it:

- Widen your stance as needed.

- Use a treat to lure your dog behind you, then between your legs.

- Feed right from your beltline if your dog is tall enough. I like to feed just above the dog's head to reward the dog for looking up at me – I think that's way cuter!

- Reward your dog for staying longer.

- Toss a treat away, then repeat.

- After 5 repetitions, lure your dog in without a treat (using an empty hand).
- Add the cue (I use "carwash") by saying it right as your dog turns back towards you from collecting the tossed treat.

8. Dog in a Box!

This shaping game is one of my all-time favorite tricks to teach your dog. It's a bit more difficult than some of the other tricks on this list, but it's worth the effort!

- Sit down in a relatively empty room with a cardboard box that's big enough for your dog. Shallow-sided boxes make things easier.

- If your dog looks at the box, moves toward the box, or makes any other sort of movement towards the box (no matter how small or accidental), click and reward. I highly recommend using a clicker for this to mark the precise moment your dog does something.

- Toss the treat away to reset your dog.

- Repeat, gradually shaping your dog towards putting his paws inside the box.

9. Paws Up

This trick is a good core workout that also helps stretch your dog's back and hips. My vet recommended that Barley does this a few times before every trail run to help loosen him up. If your dog is balancing on something unstable, it's also a great core workout!

- Start by luring your dog so his front paws are on a platform.

- Give him the cookie when he succeeds.

- Add a cue (I use "paws") and start to fade out the treat and hand motion. Barley now puts his paws on things whenever I point at them.

This trick is generally very fast to teach as long as you vary what your dog puts his paws on quickly – try your knees, the couch, a fire hydrant, stumps, and more.

10. Say Cheese (Selfie Trick)

This challenging trick is a great project for more experienced dogs and handlers. The video below explains it best – it's a bit tricky!

There are two potential approaches for teaching this trick. I'll outline the one that I found more successful here.

- Put yourself in between two objects. I used two large armchairs.

- Toss a treat behind you to get your dog behind you (inside the "funnel" you've created). Pick which arm you'll hold your phone with and which shoulder you'll want your dog to rest his chin on.

- Hold a treat over your shoulder, then lure your dog down towards your sternum. Release the treat at your sternum. If your dog struggles here, start by just feeding him at your shoulder, then your collarbone, then your sternum.

- Feed another treat behind your head.

- Repeat steps 3 and 4 until your dog is coming right back to your shoulder after the behind-the-head treat.

- Start adding the cue (I'm using "say cheese") right as your dog comes back towards your shoulder.

- Start to remove the funnel by pushing the chairs away from you, inch by inch.

You will find a list of other **_100 dog tricks_** you can teach your dog. They are here to inspire you, motivate you and get you to spend time with your dog training and ultimately creating a closer bond with your dog.

Sweet and Simple Dog Tricks

Perfect tricks to start with when you are beginning to teach your dog new things. Impressive to watch yet easy to teach these early sessions will enable you to learn about how your dog thinks and works things out before moving onto more complicated training sessions

<u>Wait</u>

The idea of this trick is to encourage calm self-control in your dog. By learning that he only gets a reward when he is calm and waits for permission then your dog will be focused to learn.

Visually pleasing to both the trainer and onlookers the wait command makes your dog appear completely obedient and tuned into the wishes of his trainer, this action is useful as a prelude to something more complicated. For a simple trick to teach, the wait command is neat and effective and extremely useful.

Dog trainers love this trick because it teaches a dog to focus and be controlled during training sessions and everyday life.

<u>Shake</u>

Shaking hands is one of the more traditional dog tricks and remarkably easy to teach. Your dog will learn to offer a front paw in response to request and solemnly shake hands with first you and then visitors to the home. Shake is an old but impressive trick to teach any dog.

Dog trainers love this trick because the shake is a great alternative to teach that prevents a dog jumping up on greeting people.

<u>Hands up</u>

Hands up is a fantastic trick that looks great. The dog is taught to sit back and hold both front paws up simultaneously. Easy to reinforce by offering the word hands up and a treat each time the dog manages to get both front paws off the ground. The pure position of this trick makes it look like it was really difficult to teach but if you reward with good timing early on then the dog will perfect his position with little effort from you.

Dog trainers love this trick because it teaches the dog focus and to concentrate on gaining a reward by getting into an unnatural position.

Speak

Teaching your dog to bark on command is easy and even more useful because you can then teach him quietness on command too.

Dog trainers love this trick and often teach it (and the next trick) in order to control a raucous barking canine.

Quiet

A natural trick to teach a dog that is fond of barking. This can be taught directly after teaching your dog to bark or as a standalone trick for a constantly woofing dog.

Dog trainers love this trick and often pass on the successful method to dog owners that are having trouble with a barking dog.

The next few tricks, although taught separately and very impressive as individual acts, can be chained together perfectly to form a practiced routine that will leave you looking and feeling like a fantastic dog trainer.

Are you tired?

Used to provoke a yawn the statement, are you tired, can give the impression that you are actually communicating with a sleepy dog. Surprisingly this is quite an easy behavior to reinforce during dog training sessions. A dog may yawn during a training session if he is confused or unsure what to do next.

This reaction is simply because yawning in the canine communication world is actually a calming signal which dogs offer when communicating with another dog or in fact any other creature at all, including human beings.

Dog trainers love this trick because it is a great example of shaping a natural behavior to give the effect of cross species communication.

Fetch your bear

Teaching you dog to fetch a particular item is pretty easy. It is just a case of showing him what the item is referred to as. In this case we will teach him to fetch a teddy bear but feel free to replace the bear with any toy that your dog may prefer.

Dog trainers love this trick because teaching a dog the name of items and to bring them for a reward has so much potential. It can work on everything from general focus to recall at the park.

Say your prayers

A fun trick that involves your dog sitting and placing his front legs onto a prop before dropping his head in apparent prayer. Once the dog knows the position, from his trick entitled hands up, he will get the idea of this one perfectly.

Dog trainers love this trick because it looks great and is quite a unique position for the dog to adopt, which encourages thought from the dog therefore providing mental stimulation.

Wave goodbye

Waving goodbye to an audience is a great trick. Even if the audience is just you it will warm your heart to see your dog waving enthusiastically towards you. Waving is a great prelude to many tricks and wonderful when you are waving to departing visitors from your front doorstep.

Dog trainers love this trick because it is another way for the dog to greet people without getting too excited and jumping up. Whilst the dog is thinking about a wave he will be focused and concentrating on the trick.

Go to bed

Great and easy to teach telling your dog to go to bed looks extremely impressive particularly when your dog is sent across a large room to seek out his sleeping quarters.

Dog trainers love this trick because as well as looking good it also provides dog owners some control within the home.

Sound asleep

A trick that, carried out well, will give the impression that your dog is fast asleep when in fact he will just be laying perfectly still waiting for his release from the position.

Dog trainers love this trick because it enables the control within the home and encourages the dog to settle, this trick can be varied when teaching your dog to settle in his bed.

So your dog has just performed his tricks perfectly. Even if you have just completed this chapter then he can tell you that he feels sleepy, fetch his teddy bear, say his prayers, wave goodbye and get into bed to fall sound asleep. That's quite an achievement. I think it's time he learned to take a bow, don't you?

Take a bow

Taking a bow is a nice trick that you can ask a dog to do after performing any other trick or routine. It is easier to teach this with the aid of a treat to lure him into the position that you can reinforce.

Dog trainers love this trick because it encourages intensive learning from the dog and also is a great addition to any other routine; the bow adds polish at the end of an already great trick.

Dance moves

A set of ten tricks that can be taught individually or as part of a sequence to create longer routines, heelwork to music has become increasingly popular and even become winning acts in TV talent shows.

These tricks will break down the wonder that is a dancing dog into easy stages for you to learn with your pet.

Reverse

The act of the dog walking backwards whilst facing his handler, this is made even neater if the handler simultaneously walks towards the dog which gives the impression of dancing.

Dog trainers love this trick because it teaches the dog to focus his mind on his handler whilst also carrying out another physical task.

Twist

Twist is a great trick which consists of teaching a dog to spin, on all four feet, in a circle in front of his handler.

Dog trainers love this trick because it's easy to teach and great to lift the confidence of a dog in training.

Target stick

A target stick is a great prop for a heelwork to music with your dog. It can be incorporated into the routine as a walking stick or umbrella. A target stick is brilliant for both directing your dog and as part of other more complicated tricks.

If your dog is targeted to the end of a stick he will follow it with his eyes and body in order to attempt to provoke a reward from you. This is an impressive act alone but will also open many doors for training further tricks.

Dog trainers love targeting a canine to a stick because it opens up so many options when training a dog to do tricks.

Pick up stick

Any dog that will pick up a walking stick and pass it to his handler is impressive. Added to a dance routine it can be even more remarkable. This trick can be easily achieved by expanding on the previous targeting technique.

Dog trainers love this trick because teaching a dog to pick up any item is simply a prelude to the dog picking up many more items, this can be a very useful exercise.

Commando

A dog that crawls along on his belly is easy to teach even though this looks like a complicated trick.

Dog trainers love this trick because it is simple to teach yet looks like a complicated behavior. The dog can then be taught to crawl under things, which is also an extremely cute trick.

Roll Over

A dog that is laying down in front of you can easily and quickly be taught to roll over onto his back then return to his stomach in a quick 360 degree turn. A quick trick that can fit in perfectly with many other maneuvers

Dog trainers love this trick because it can also be used to teach a dog to roll in his blanket, an impressive enhancement to canine bedtime

Weave

This trick looks very intense and is indeed an expert example of teamwork; a walking handler is joined by a keen dog weaving through his master legs.

Dog trainers love this trick because it looks so smooth and easy when perfected.

Circle me

A trick that involves the dog circling his master's body, this looks neat and is very impressive.

Dog trainers love this trick because it is easy to teach but can be added to a sequence of heel work or obedience to add flair to any routine.

Stand tall

A great trick that can be physically taxing for older or less fit dogs, this trick is for the fittest and most physically capable of canines. For this trick your dog will learn to stand on his rear legs.

Dog trainers love this trick because it improves a dog's stamina and focus.

Walk tall

This is a variation of the stand tall exercise, a dog that has perfected balance is then asked to walk on his back legs.

Dog trainers love this trick because it improves focus, balance and stamina for a dog. It is also quite challenging on dog training ability.

A dog that can help around the house is a delight, even more so when you can show his skills off to your friends and family.

Shut the door

This is quite a popular trick and surprisingly easy to teach. Your dog will learn how to close an open door when asked to do so.

Dog trainers love this trick because it utilizes a fantastic positive training technique which is targeting with positive reinforcement.

Open the Door

A trick that teaches your dog to open a door, some dogs may need a little help with this due to size and handle type, a dog that can open a door on command will impress everyone in the room.

Dog trainer's love this trick because when your dog can open a door this can progress to more impressive acts.

Fetch the TV Remote

A trick that can be used every day, teach your dog to fetch the TV remote and you will never lose it again. Prepare for a soggy remote if you have a particularly slobbery dog.

Dog trainers love this trick because it can be utilized in many ways in order to train a dog to retrieve almost anything.

Pick up keys

A fantastic trick taught to service dogs that live with disabled and older people. Your dog will see that you have dropped your keys and pick them up from the ground to pass back to you.

For this trick it may help that you have a cute or plush key ring, even some knotted material on your key fob will help your dog to lift and carry your keys. This trick does not necessarily need a command word for it calls to the initiative of your dog.

Dog trainers love this trick because it is teaching a dog to use his initiative when he sees your keys drop to the ground.

Find Keys

An extension of the previously taught trick of picking up dropped keys, the find keys trick is most useful if keys are dropped out walking or lost in the home.

Dog trainers love this trick because it is one of the most useful things a dog can do and is also really easy to teach.

Fetch the newspaper

A great and most useful trick, your dog could easily learn that bringing you the newspaper is one of his daily tasks.

Dog trainers love this trick because it is a great way to teach a positive response to the mailman.

Differentiate between items

There is no command to this trick because each item will have its own command word. However, if you have a bone, bear and ball and would like your dog to recognize each by name then this is the trick for you.

Dog trainers love this trick because it appears truly skillful to train a dog to pick out one particular item by name when faced with many.

Wake up

This is a truly heartwarming trick used by dog trainers when teaching a dog to respond to the alarm clock and wake a deaf person in a morning. You can teach your dog to do this too although it will take time and patience it is great fun and very rewarding.

Dog trainers love this trick because it's a great experience to be woken by a keen and loving canine rather than the electronic sound of an alarm clock.

Pass a note

This is a fun trick for all of the family. Writing a note and passing it to the dog to take to someone in another room is great.

Dog trainers love this trick because it can be easily modified and a dog can be a useful addition to a busy household by enhancing communication in a fun way.

Fetch a drink

Having your dog fetch you a drink from a fridge or cupboard is entertaining and when he knows how to open a door it's not so difficult to teach

Dog trainer's love this trick because trained carefully most dogs can be taught to fetch a cold drink from the fridge for their owners.

Household chores

Surprisingly easy to teach tricks that also ensure your dog helps around the house as much as possible.

Wipe your paws

Great for cleaning off muddy paws after a walk, you can teach your dog to wipe his paws on a mat at the front door before entering the house.

Dog trainers love this trick because it utilizes the natural behavior of a dog and is helpful after long muddy walks, perfect for multi dog homes.

Shake

A dog that shakes on command is both useful and fun to watch. This is a natural behavior for a dog with a wet coat so not difficult to reinforce but looks great when performed by a dry dog. You can utilize this trick after a wet walk to keep water out of the house.

Dog trainers love this trick because this is truly dog training by positive reinforcement alone.

Put your toys away

Teaching your dog to put his toys away is very rewarding. Watching him gather everything into a box when asked is impressive and will make you proud.

Dog trainers love this trick because it really makes the dog think about the goal to get his reward.

Fetch the phone

A dog that will fetch the phone when it rings is a really useful trick to teach. Dog trainers love this trick because it is useful and very impressive.

Take off your socks

Fun and impressive, the act of your dog taking off your socks never gets old. Dog trainers love this trick because playing tug raises the confidence of a sensitive dog.

Unzip your jacket

Fantastic fun, a dog that helps you off with your coat as you walk into a room is a really impressive trick.

Dog trainers love this trick because it encourages focus from the dog on greeting therefore prevents over excitement.

Laundry basket

Fantastic and useful, teach your dog to put the laundry into the basket and he will certainly be earning his biscuits. This trick is similar to putting his toys away and a great addition to removing your socks or jacket.

Dog trainers love this trick because it provides a base for many other tricks

Close the curtains

Teach your dog to close the curtains and impress visitors every time he does it on command.

Dog trainers love this trick because it is fun and is a little unusual.

The agility Dog

Tricks that teach your dog to be agile which are also really impressive to watch. It's important that your dog is fit and healthy for these tricks; they are perfect for wearing out a bouncy dog.

Hurdle

This is fun! Teaching your dog to jump over hurdles is addictive, a big part of competitive agility training hurdles will both use up your dogs' energy and encourage him to focus on you.

Dog trainers love this trick because it encourages focus whilst improving stamina and fitness.

Bounce

The dog that will bounce spritely in the air again and again looks amazing. Jumping on the spot is a trick that could easily make your dog look like he is on springs. A great and fun act to watch and encourage.

Dog trainers love this trick because it's a challenge as it's not a natural behavior to teach to most dogs.

Hop it

This trick is really impressive and can be used as a standalone trick or part of a routine. You will need your target stick for this as you are going to hold it for your dog to jump over.

Dog trainers love this trick because it is so neat and versatile. It is also often utilized in heelwork to music and enhanced obedience routines.

Sneaky

Sneaky is a trick that is quite simple but can look great in many situations. Being sneaky is just asking your dog to go underneath something. For this trick we will teach him to crawl underneath a low hurdle but when your dog knows the command you can apply it to going under anything.

Dog trainers love this trick because it can be utilized in so many ways, when your dog knows the command, sneaky, you can direct him under any obstacle.

Weave poles

Weave poles can be taught quickly and easily by luring a dog through them with either a treat or target stick. Used as part of competitive agility a dog flying with speed and agility through a set of poles is an impressive act.

Dog trainers love this trick, particularly in competitive agility sessions as the dogs thoroughly enjoy the weave.

Through the hole

Fantastic and fun this trick is one of the most impressive agility acts to teach. Whilst you stand side on to your pet and create a loop with your arms the dog jumps directly through the loop. No one can fail to be impressed!

Dog trainers love this trick because it is the ultimate in team work and also looks brilliant to spectators.

Jump into your arms

A dog that will trust enough to jump directly into his handlers' arms is a happy dog. This trick will consist of your dog jumping up into your waiting arms whilst you catch him. This is a nice stand-alone trick or good as part of a longer routine.

Dog trainers love this trick because it enhances trust in the relationship with their canine.

Hoop

This trick consists of the dog jumping through a hoop held at any height or angle. The hoop can be suspended in the air or held by the handler.

Dog trainers love this trick because it can be a challenge to teach and it also builds human/canine trust.

The moving hoop

An extension of jumping through a hoop this trick requires some skill mainly on the part of the trainer. You will pass the hoop from your left to right and because your dog knows the command he will jump through it both times.

Dog trainers love this trick because it is the ultimate teamwork and quite a good workout on the arms for the trainer too.

Leap me

Your dog will jump over the back of a person on their hands and knees when performing this trick. When the command is learned it can be extended in order for your dog to jump over you. This is a great trick to add into any routine.

Dog trainers love this trick because it improves stamina in a dog and trust between dog and trainer.

The working dog

Dogs are employed throughout the world to do many jobs. These tricks will give you an idea of how they are trained in some common roles, and also give your dog a taste of the working life.

Find it!

All search tasks are first based in retrieve. In fact, to a sniffer dog the entire search process is a prelude to a game of retrieve. Fetching something and bringing it back on command is a nice trick that comes in useful both alone and as the beginning of further routines.

Dog trainers love retrieve games because they exercise, stimulate and offer control to a dog all at once.

Present!

Present is a useful trick for a dog that likes to hold on to a toy and not give it back to you. Your dog will learn to come to you with a toy in his mouth and sit before offering you the opportunity to take the toy from him.

Dog trainers love the retrieve and present as it encourages focus on the toy on walks and during training sessions.

Search tricks to impress

The following tricks are based on search techniques used in professional dog training organizations. The information is simply to give you a taster and help you to entertain yourself and your dog you will have a lot of fun and enjoy the results of this training. The same command word is fine to be used for all of the search tricks, seek or find are good examples of search commands.

Use your nose

Encouraging your dog to use his nose is a learning process for both of you. This trick is a good way to teach scenting to find a toy which also looks great to an audience

Dog trainers love this trick because it teaches focus and control to a dog.

Room

A trick that consists of your dog searching a room to find his toy, with practice your dog will be able to sniff out his toy in cupboards and at any height. To train this trick you may need a helper to hold your dog so that he can watch you hide the toy.

Dog trainers love this trick because it uses a dog's energy up both mentally and physically.

Garden

Searching the garden for a toy is a great trick particularly at barbeques where your dog can show off his expertise in style.

Dog trainers love this trick, it's great for stamina, focus and any dog that can search is a crowd pleaser.

Route

Searching a route originates from gaining security clearance along roads or through built up areas. It is not safe to do this search in traffic. However, if you regularly walk up a quiet lane or similar, searching the walking route for his toy will give your dog a good physical and mental workout.

Dog trainers love this trick because it is great for physical fitness and stamina of a dog.

Vehicle

A dog that searches the outside of a vehicle for his toy is impressive. This is a fun trick for party parking, your own vehicle security dog.

Dog trainers love this trick because it looks professional and encourages the dog to think.

A group of people

Often seen at airports and similar environments the dog that can search a group of people is a head turner. A great trick again to have at parties and for this trick you will need a group of willing volunteers to practice on.

Dog trainers love this trick because it's professional and encourages the dog to work hard with his nose.

Track a person

Tracking a person at the park is another trick that your dog will need to use his nose for. You will need a helper for this. Teaching a dog to track is great fun.

Dog trainers love this trick because it will wear out even the most energetic of dogs.

Patience

The passive response is the act of the dog asking nicely for his toy. This is taught in situations where a search dog is scenting for explosives and must not touch the area of his find. As a dog trick this can be called "ask nicely" or "patience"

Dog trainers love this trick because it teaches focus perfectly.

Crowd Pleasers

A selection of dog tricks that everyone enjoys which are also surprisingly easy to teach. All of these tricks can be taught by using positive reinforcement and the following pages will show you how.

Give a paw

Few people greet a dog without asking for a paw, this trick is as old as the sit request but a dog that gives a paw on command will always bring a smile.

Dog trainers love this classic trick particularly taught with positive reinforcement.

Swap the paw

When your dog is giving you a paw a great spin is to ask for the other paw instead. This is another trick that will come quite naturally to your dog. It will become established with reinforcement.

Dog trainers love this trick because it looks neat and encourages the dog to think for reward.

Both paws

A wonderful trick that looks lovely. The dog will get into the sit position and place both paws onto you for a reward. This is another trick that may take some thinking on your dog's part but once established he will be offering the behavior at every opportunity

Dog trainers love this trick as it's an interesting twist on the classic shake a paw trick.

Kisses

Teach your dog to give a big kiss on command. Kiss is a lovely and fun trick to try out on yourself and others.

Dog trainers love this trick because it is great fun and easy to teach.

Look left

A fascinating trick that will impress even the most skeptical of audiences, teach your dog to look left on command and anyone can be forgiven for appreciating his grasp on the English language.

Dog trainers love this trick because it needs excellent timing to teach and can only be taught by positive reinforcement.

Look right

A trick that teaches the dog to look right on command, this looks fantastic when used with the previous trick of looking left on command.

Dog trainers love this trick because dog training is always improved by the necessity of applying excellent timing.

No

A trick that gives the impression that your dog is saying no when asked a question.

Dog trainers love this trick because it uses excellent timing to chain together tricks that are already taught.

Sky

This trick consists of your dog looking upwards towards the sky. Most dogs are limited in how far they can point their nose into the air so keep this in mind whilst teaching this trick.

Dog trainers love this trick because it takes skill, patience and concentration to teach.

Ground

This trick will teach your dog to look at the ground on command. This response is fantastic for persuading an audience that your dog knows exactly what you are saying.

Dog trainers love this trick because it is so easy to teach using positive reinforcement and its great fun to watch a dog work out what to do for his reward.

Yes

Say yes is a trick that will impress even the most doubting of audiences. A dog that can nod when asked if he wants a biscuit is fantastic fun.

Dog trainers love this trick because it is a challenge to teach and will improve timing during dog training sessions.

Wolf

Teach your dog to howl like a wolf and show off a trick that is both endearing and impressive.

A dog trainer loves this trick because dogs howl sounds wonderful, and is amazingly cute.

Singing star

Similar to howling but this trick ensures that your dog sings along with you so you can offer a fantastic duet to an appreciative audience.

Dog trainers love this trick because it is fun and a great stress reliever.

Growly bear

Teach your dog to growl on command.

Dog trainers love this trick because it's unusual to see a dog growling at his handler in order to obtain a treat.

Whistle

Teach your dog to come running keenly when he hears the sound of a whistle. Dog trainers love this trick because it enhances canine recall.

Stand still

A trick that enables you to tell your dog to stand completely still, this act will help your dog to disregard anything that is going on around him.

Dog trainers love this trick because it combines focus and concentration for both dog and trainer.

Fetch his bowl

Fetching a bowl is an excellent trick where your dog fetches his food bowl to ask you to fill it with food. This looks great however you may be fending off a hungry dog more often than you would like.

Dog trainers love this trick because a hungry and persistent dog will never allow you to forget their meal.

High five

High five is a trick that is an extension from giving a paw and wave goodbye.

Dog trainers love this trick because it is great at the end of a combined routine.

Balance

The ultimate in self-control is a dog that will hold a biscuit on his nose and then give it back unharmed. This trick will help you to teach your dog just that!

Dog trainers love this trick because it encourages control and focus.

Stay

Teaching this trick will ensure that your dog learns to stay completely still when you ask him to stay despite what is going on around him.

Dog trainers love this trick because it offers control in busy situations.

Statue

This is a stay where you can go out of sight but the dog will not move. This stay is a good trick to first practice in the garden and perfect at the park.

Dog trainers love this trick because it enhances trust and provides control. Cute tricks for the cutest dogs.

A group of cute and classic dog tricks which you will never get tired of.

Fetch my slippers

A classic trick with the twist of being taught by positive reinforcement. A dog that will fetch your slippers is useful and fun.

Dog trainers love this classic trick because it is useful and extremely cute.

Fetch your leash

Every dog should be able to fetch his leash when asked. In fact, if you teach this trick to your dog don't be surprised if he fetches it whether he has been asked or not.

Dog trainers love this trick because it is classic and never ages.

Make friends

This is one of the most endearing tricks which your dog can learn and perform. He will approach someone gently and place his head in their lap or on their leg. Offering friendship as only a dog does.

Dog trainer's love this trick because it encourages gentle greeting from even the bounciest of dogs.

Smile

A dog that smiles is funny and incredibly cute. Some offer a submissive smile naturally which is easy to reinforce. The important thing about this trick is to recognize your dog's individual smile and shape it with reinforcement.

Dog trainers love this trick because it can be a challenge to teach, and dog trainers love a challenge.

Laugh

Most dogs make a snuffling noise when they become excited. It's not quite a sneeze and most often occurs when you have one to one contact with your dog. This sound is best described as laughter. The trick of asking your dog to laugh is wonderful to witness because you can really tell that he is having fun .

Dog trainers love this trick because it's unusual and wonderful to see a dog laughing.

Get busy

Get busy is an extremely useful trick because this is the act of toileting outside on command, which will help you extensively when short of time on walks.

Dog trainers love this trick because it's extremely useful to use before training sessions.

Bang

Bang is fun, cute and universally entertaining. The dog shot by an imaginary gun drops to the floor and plays dead for an audience.

Dog trainers love this trick because when well- practiced it looks great and is also easy to teach.

Touch your nose

This trick consists of your dog lifting his paw and touching his nose on command.

Dog trainers love this trick because it is another trick that offers the suggestion that your dog speaks your language.

Ashamed

This trick teaches your dog to lie on the ground and put his paw over his muzzle as if ashamed or in trouble.

Dog trainers love this trick because it looks extremely cute and takes some concentration to train.

Sore paw

This trick is great to fool unsuspecting visitors as your dog will lift his paw into the air feigning injury.

Dog trainers love this trick because dog and trainer can work as a team to provoke a sympathetic reaction from any onlooker.

Go around it

This trick involves your dog going around any obstacle on command this can include the sofa, car or even a lake on a walk.

Dog trainers love this trick because it's original and fun.

Catch

Your dog will happily catch treats all day, this trick will teach him to catch more unusual objects.

Dog trainers love this trick because it encourages alertness and focus.

Nose nudge

This trick is wonderful. It is taught to assistance dogs as a way to get their handlers attention by applying a gentle nudge from the nose.

Dog trainers love this trick because it is teaching your dog a non-invasive and gentle way to ask for your attention.

Touch with paw

This trick is teaching your dog the act of touching an item with his paw. This can come in handy for many things from switching on a light to ringing a bell.

Dog trainers love this trick because targeting to a disk enables the dog to touch any object with little further training.

Doorbell

The ultimate dog trick is ringing a doorbell to come back into the house from the garden.

Dog trainers love this trick because it encourages a dog to use his initiative. Coordinated canine

Some advanced tricks that you can add to a routine which provide pure flair! These next tricks utilize the use of your target stick.

Rear leg twirl

This is a physically demanding trick that must only be carried out by a dog that has physically sound hips and rear legs. He will learn to stand up on his rear legs and twirl in a circle; it looks impressive and is great fun.

Dog trainers love this trick because it is amazing to watch and extremely impressive.

Loop the loop

This trick is fun and consists of your dog spinning quickly in a continuous circle on all four feet until released from the trick.

Dog trainers love this trick because it uses up canine energy and looks fantastic.

All change

All change is a trick where the dog loops first one way and then the other; it looks great and due to the change in direction is extremely impressive.

Dog trainers love this trick because it requires focus during intense physical activity.

Twirl stick

This trick looks pretty and is great as part of an enhanced obedience routine. Your dog will quickly complete a loop around your target stick.

Dog trainers love this trick because it is great fun ad a wonderful use of a prop to complete and impressive canine freestyle routine.

Freeze

A perfect final trick to teach your dog is the freeze. Your dog will literally become a statue in whichever position he is in at the time and not move until released.

Dog trainers love this trick because it requires the ultimate timing and skill to teach.

FUNNY DOG QUOTES

"Outside of a dog, a book is a man's best friend. Inside of a dog it's too dark to read." – Groucho Marx

"My fashion philosophy is, if you're not covered in dog hair, your life is empty." – Elayne Boosler

"No one appreciates the very special genius of your conversation as the dog does." – Christopher Morley

"Dog is God spelled backward." – Duane Chapman

"Scratch a dog and you'll find a permanent job." – Franklin P. Jones

"A boy can learn a lot from a dog: obedience, loyalty, and the importance of turning around three times before lying down." – Robert Benchley

"When a man's best friend is his dog, that dog has a problem." – Edward Abbey

"Dogs have boundless enthusiasm but no sense of shame. I should have a dog as a life coach." – Moby

"You want a friend in Washington? Get a dog." – Harry S Truman

"The dog is the god of frolic." – Henry Ward Beecher

"Anybody who doesn't know what soap tastes like never washed a dog." – Franklin P. Jones

"What do dogs do on their day off? Can't lie around – that's their job." – George Carlin

"I don't understand people who don't touch their pets. Their cat or dog is called a pet for a reason." – Jarod Kintz

"If you don't own a dog, at least one, there is not necessarily anything wrong with you, but there may be something wrong with your life." – Roger A. Caras

"All his life he tried to be a good person. Many times, however, he failed. For after all, he was only human. He wasn't a dog." – Charles M Schulz

"I like dogs. You always know what a dog is thinking. It has four moods. Happy, sad, cross, and concentrating. Also, dogs are faithful and they do not tell lies because they cannot talk." – Mark Haddon

"I've seen a look in dogs' eyes, a quickly vanishing look of amazed contempt, and I am convinced that basically dogs think humans are nuts." – John Steinbeck

"They [dogs] never talk about themselves but listen to you while you talk about yourself, and keep up an appearance of being interested in the conversation." – Jerome K. Jerome

ABOUT THE AUTHOR

David Bobker is a prolific author who has published over 30 books under several pen names. His purpose as an author is to enlighten and help people through his books.

Previously David has been an Advisory Director at Argyle, Senior Vice President of AST Phoenix Advisors, Managing Director with Georgeson and was one of the founders of Laurel Hill Advisors.

A 1993 graduate of the City University of New York's Brooklyn College with a Bachelor's degree in Computer Science, David earned his MBA in Marketing and Finance from the City University of New York's Baruch College in 2000. David lives with his wife Shoshana, a certified nutritionist, and their seven children in Passaic, New Jersey.